DIVIDEND INVESTING

The Beginners Guide To
Dividend Investing

Benjamin J. Mornington

Copyright © 2023 LUL LTD

All rights reserved

The characters and events portrayed in this book are fictitious. Any similarity to real persons, living or dead, is coincidental and not intended by the author.

No part of this book may be reproduced, or stored in a retrieval system, or transmitted in any form or by any means, electronic, mechanical, photocopying, recording, or otherwise, without express written permission of the publisher.

ISBN-13: 9798375492865

Cover design by: Art Painter
Library of Congress Control Number: 2018675309
Printed in the United States of America

CONTENTS

Title Page

Copyright

Disclaimer — 1

Chapter 1: Introduction — 2

Explanation of what dividends are and why they are important to investors — 4

Overview of the book's content and goals — 7

Chapter 2: Understanding Dividend Paying Stocks — 10

What are Blue Chip Stocks? — 11

Understanding Real Estate Investment Trusts (REITs) — 14

Master Limited Partnerships (MLPs) — 17

Dividend Calculation and Payment — 20

The Impact of Dividends on Stock Prices — 23

Chapter 3: Dividend Investing Strategies — 26

Dividend Growth Investing — 28

Dividend Income Investing	31
Dividend Yield Investing	34
Selecting the Right Dividend Investing Strategy - At A Glance	37
Chapter 4: Risk Management and Dividend Investing	40
Risks Associated with Dividend Investing	42
Managing Risks in Dividend Investing	45
Chapter 5: Tax Implications of Dividend Investing	48
Minimizing Taxes on Dividends	51
Analysis of How Tax Laws and Regulations Affect Dividend Investing	54
Chapter 6: The Impact of Low-Interest Rates on Dividend Investing	57
Finding Dividend-Paying Stocks in a Low-Interest Rate Environment	60
Bond and Fixed Income Investments in a Dividend Investing Strategy	63
Chapter 7: Dividend Investing in International Markets	67
Finding and Researching International Dividend-Paying Stocks	69
Diversifying Your Dividend Portfolio with International Stocks	75
Chapter 8: The Dividend Snowball - The Power of Compound Dividend Growth	78

What is the Dividend Snowball?	79
The Power of Compound Growth:	80
Examples of the Dividend Snowball:	81
The Importance of Reinvesting Dividends:	82
Chapter 9: Why Warren Buffet Loves Dividends	84
Chapter 10: Conclusion - The Power of Dividend Investing	87
Discussion of ongoing research and trends in dividend investing	89
Final thoughts and recommendations for investors.	92
Afterword	95

DISCLAIMER

Disclaimer: The author of this book is not a licensed financial professional and the information contained within is not intended to be taken as financial advice. Investing in stocks and other securities carries a risk of loss. Please consult a licensed financial advisor and conduct your own research before making any investment decisions.

It is also important to consult with a tax professional when dealing with tax implications of investing, especially when it comes to reporting, as tax laws and rules may vary depending on the country or state and the circumstances.

CHAPTER 1: INTRODUCTION

Dividend investing is a strategy that focuses on buying stocks that pay regular dividends to their shareholders. Dividends are payments made by a company to its shareholders, usually on a quarterly basis. They can be in the form of cash or stock and are typically a percentage of the company's earnings.

Dividend investing is popular among investors for several reasons. First, dividends provide a steady stream of income, which can be especially valuable for retirees or other investors who are seeking regular cash flow. Second, dividends can be a sign of a company's financial health and stability. Companies that consistently pay dividends are typically more established and have a track record of profitable operations. Third, dividends can provide a level of downside protection for stock investors.

In times of market volatility or recession, dividends can provide some cushion for the value of the stock.

However, dividend investing is not without its risks. Dividends can be cut or eliminated, and companies that pay high dividends may be overvalued or have a less favorable outlook. It is important for investors to thoroughly research a company before investing in its stock, and to diversify their portfolio to manage risk.

In this book, we will explore the various aspects of dividend investing in greater detail. We will discuss different types of dividend-paying stocks, different dividend-investing strategies, risk management, and tax implications. Additionally, we will examine the impact of low-interest rates on dividend investing and how to invest in dividends in international markets. By the end of this book, readers will have a comprehensive understanding of dividend investing and the tools they need to make informed investment decisions.

EXPLANATION OF WHAT DIVIDENDS ARE AND WHY THEY ARE IMPORTANT TO INVESTORS

Dividends are payments made by a company to its shareholders, typically on a quarterly basis. They can be in the form of cash or stock and are usually a percentage of the company's earnings. Dividends are an important aspect of stock investing, as they can provide a steady stream of income for investors.

When a company earns a profit, it has a few options

for what to do with that money. It can retain the profits and use them to reinvest in the business, pay off debt, or make acquisitions. Alternatively, the company can distribute a portion of the profits to shareholders in the form of dividends. When a company pays dividends, it is essentially sharing some of its profits with its investors.

There are several reasons why dividends are important to stock investors. First, dividends provide a steady stream of income, which can be especially valuable for investors who are seeking regular cash flow. Second, dividends can be a sign of a company's financial health and stability. Companies that consistently pay dividends are typically more established and have a track record of profitable operations. Third, dividends can provide a level of downside protection for stock investors. In times of market volatility or recession, dividends can provide some cushion for the value of the stock.

However, it's also important to keep in mind that not all companies pay dividends, and not all dividends are created equal. Some companies may have a history of consistently paying dividends, while others may only pay dividends occasionally or not at all. Additionally, some dividends may be larger or more consistent than others. As an investor, it's important to research a company's dividend history and payout ratio before investing in its stock.

Additionally, it is important to note that dividends

are taxed at the federal and state level, so investors should consider the tax implications when planning their investment strategies.

In summary, dividends are payments made by a company to its shareholders, typically on a quarterly basis. They provide a steady stream of income and can be a sign of a company's financial health and stability. Dividends can also provide downside protection for stock investors. However, not all companies pay dividends and not all dividends are created equal, so investors should research a company's dividend history and payout ratio before investing in its stock.

OVERVIEW OF THE BOOK'S CONTENT AND GOALS

The world of dividend investing can be a complex one, with a multitude of options and strategies available for individual investors. Whether you're a seasoned investor or just starting out, it's important to understand the basics of this type of investment and how it can be used to build a secure financial future. This book aims to provide a comprehensive overview of everything you need to know about dividend investing, from the basics of what dividends are and why they are important, to more advanced topics like international dividend investing and risk management.

Goals:

The main goals of this book are to:

1. Provide a clear and concise understanding of what dividend investing is and how it works.

2. Discuss the various types of dividend-paying stocks, including blue-chip stocks, REITs, and MLPs.

3. Explore the different dividend investing strategies, including dividend growth investing, income investing, and yield investing, and provide guidance on how to choose the right one for your needs.

4. Discuss the risks associated with dividend investing and provide strategies for managing those risks.

5. Explain the tax implications of dividend investing and the benefits of compounding your dividends over time.

6. Offer an overview of ongoing research and trends in the world of dividend investing.

7. Provide guidance on how to find and research international dividend-paying stocks, and how to diversify a dividend-investing portfolio with international stocks.

Throughout this book, you will find real-world

examples and case studies to help illustrate the concepts and strategies discussed, making it an essential resource for anyone looking to build a successful dividend investing portfolio.

CHAPTER 2: UNDERSTANDING DIVIDEND PAYING STOCKS

When it comes to dividend investing, there are several different types of stocks that investors can choose from. Each type has its own set of characteristics and potential risks and rewards. Here, we'll take a look at three popular types of dividend-paying stocks: blue-chip stocks, Real Estate Investment Trusts (REITs), and Master Limited Partnerships (MLPs).

WHAT ARE BLUE CHIP STOCKS?

A blue-chip stock is a stock of a well-established, large company that has a history of paying dividends. These stocks are typically considered to be less risky than other types of stocks, as they tend to be more stable and have a consistent track record of profitability.

Blue chip stocks are often associated with companies in the Dow Jones Industrial Average (DJIA), a stock market index that includes 30 of the largest and most well-known companies in the United States. Examples of blue chip stocks include Coca-Cola, Procter & Gamble, and Johnson & Johnson. These companies have a long history of profitability and have been paying dividends for decades.

Blue chip stocks are often considered to be a safe investment, as they tend to be less volatile than other types of stocks. This is because they are typically well-established companies with a strong track record of profitability. Additionally, blue chip stocks are considered to be less risky because they are less likely to go bankrupt or experience significant financial difficulties.

However, it's important to note that even blue-chip stocks can be affected by market downturns or economic recessions. Additionally, the dividends of blue chip stocks may fluctuate over time, depending on the company's financial performance.

One of the advantages of blue chip stocks is that they tend to be less affected by market volatility than other types of stocks. They also provide a steady stream of dividends, which can provide a source of income for investors. Additionally, blue chip stocks tend to be more stable in the long term and may be less likely to experience significant price fluctuations.

Despite these advantages, blue chip stocks also have some disadvantages. They tend to be more expensive than other types of stocks, which can make them less accessible for some investors. Additionally, blue chip stocks may not offer as much potential for capital appreciation as other types of stocks.

In summary, a blue chip stock is a stock of a well-established, large company that has a history of paying dividends. Blue chip stocks are typically considered to be less risky than other types of stocks and may provide a steady stream of dividends. They are more stable in the long term and may be less likely to experience significant price fluctuations. However, they also tend to be more expensive and may not offer as much potential for capital appreciation.

UNDERSTANDING REAL ESTATE INVESTMENT TRUSTS (REITS)

A Real Estate Investment Trust (REIT) is a type of security that allows individuals to invest in a diversified portfolio of income-producing real estate assets. REITs are required by law to distribute at least 90% of their taxable income to shareholders in the form of dividends. This makes REITs an attractive investment option for those looking for regular income streams.

REITs can invest in a variety of real estate assets, including office buildings, apartments, hotels, shopping centers, and warehouses. They may also invest in mortgages, mortgage-backed securities, and other real estate-related assets. REITs can be publicly traded on stock exchanges or privately held.

One of the main advantages of REITs is that they provide investors with a way to invest in real estate without the hassle and expense of buying and managing the property themselves. REITs are also highly liquid, meaning that shares can be easily bought and sold on stock exchanges.

Additionally, REITs can provide diversification benefits, as they allow investors to spread their investments across a variety of different real estate assets and sectors. This can help to mitigate risk and provide a more stable income stream.

However, there are some disadvantages to REITs as well. REITs are generally considered to be riskier than bonds and other fixed-income investments, so they may not be suitable for all investors. Additionally, REITs are also subject to fluctuations in the value of the underlying real estate assets, which can affect the value of the REIT's shares.

It's important to note that REITs are also subject to tax implications, especially those that are publicly traded. Dividends paid by REITs are taxed as ordinary income, which can be higher than the tax on capital gains or qualified dividends. Therefore, investors should consult with their tax advisors before investing in REITs.

In summary, Real Estate Investment Trusts (REITs) are a type of security that allows individuals to invest in a diversified portfolio of income-producing real estate assets. REITs provide regular income streams through dividends and offer investors the opportunity to invest in real estate without the hassle and expense of buying and managing the property themselves. Additionally, REITs can provide diversification benefits, however, they also come with higher risk than bonds and other fixed-income investments and are subject to fluctuations in the value of the underlying real estate assets.

MASTER LIMITED PARTNERSHIPS (MLPS)

Master Limited Partnerships (MLPs) are a unique type of publicly traded security that is typically involved in the energy sector, such as pipeline companies, and oil and gas exploration and production companies. These companies are organized as partnerships, rather than corporations, and are required to pay out the majority of their income to investors in the form of dividends. MLPs are designed to provide investors with a steady stream of income, while also providing tax benefits.

One of the main advantages of MLPs is that they often have a high yield, making them an attractive option for income-oriented investors. For example, the average yield for MLPs is around 6%, compared to the average yield for the S&P 500 of around 2%. This high yield can provide investors with a significant source of income that can help to meet their financial goals.

Another advantage of MLPs is that they can provide investors with a way to participate in the energy sector without having to directly own the underlying assets. MLPs typically own and operate energy infrastructure assets, such as pipelines and storage facilities, that are critical to the transportation and distribution of energy products. By investing in an MLP, investors can gain exposure to the energy sector without having to directly own the assets.

Despite their advantages, MLPs also comes with certain risks. One of the main risks is that MLPs are typically more complex than other types of stocks, and investors should be aware of the tax implications before investing. MLPs are considered pass-through entities, which means that they do not pay corporate income taxes. Instead, the income is passed through to the investors, who are then responsible for paying taxes on their share of the income. This can make MLPs more difficult to understand and manage from a tax perspective.

Another risk to consider is that MLPs are heavily dependent on the energy sector, which can be affected by a variety of factors, such as changes in commodity prices, economic conditions, and government regulations. This can make the performance of MLPs highly correlated to the performance of the energy sector, which can be highly volatile.

It's important to note that MLPs may not be suitable for all investors, and investors should carefully consider their own risk tolerance, investment goals, and diversification strategy before investing in MLPs. As always, it's important to conduct thorough research and consult with a financial advisor before making any investment decisions.

In summary, Master Limited Partnerships (MLPs) are a unique type of publicly traded security that is typically involved in the energy sector. They are organized as partnerships, rather than corporations, and are required to pay out the majority of their income to investors in the form of dividends. MLPs offer high yields and provide investors with a way to participate in the energy sector without having to directly own the underlying assets. However, they also come with certain risks, such as tax implications and high correlation with the energy sector. Investors should carefully consider their own risk tolerance, investment goals, and diversification strategy before investing in MLPs.

DIVIDEND CALCULATION AND PAYMENT

Dividends are payments made by a company to its shareholders, usually on a quarterly or annual basis. These payments are typically made in cash, but can also be made in the form of stock or other assets. The amount of the dividend payment is determined by the company's board of directors and is based on the company's earnings and financial position.

There are several different ways that dividends can be calculated, but the most common method is through the use of a payout ratio. A payout ratio is the percentage of earnings that a company pays out as dividends. For example, if a company has earnings per share (EPS) of $1 and pays out a dividend of $0.50 per share, the payout ratio would be 50%.

The payout ratio is an important metric for investors because it indicates the company's willingness and ability to pay dividends. A high payout ratio may indicate that the company is committed to paying dividends, but it may also indicate that the company is not reinvesting enough of its earnings to support future growth. On the other hand, a low payout ratio may indicate that the company has more flexibility to reinvest its earnings or increase dividends in the future.

Once the dividend amount is determined, it is paid out to shareholders on the dividend record date. The dividend record date is the date on which a company's shareholders are recorded in the company's books as the owners of the stock, and are therefore entitled to receive the dividend. Shareholders who own the stock on the record date, known as the "ex-dividend date," will receive the dividend payment.

It's also worth noting that companies also have different types of dividends

- Regular dividends: These dividends are the most common and are paid out on a regular schedule, such as quarterly or annually.
- Special dividends: These dividends are paid out in addition to regular dividends and are usually one-time payments. Special dividends are often paid out when a company has a large amount of

cash on hand or when a company's stock price is high.

- Dividend Reinvestment Plan (DRIP): Some companies allow shareholders to reinvest their dividends back into the company's stock, rather than receiving cash payments. This is known as a Dividend Reinvestment Plan (DRIP).

In conclusion, dividends are payments made by a company to its shareholders, usually on a quarterly or annual basis. The amount of the dividend payment is determined by the company's board of directors and is based on the company's earnings and financial position. The payout ratio is an important metric for investors because it indicates the company's willingness and ability to pay dividends. Companies also have different types of dividends, such as regular dividends, special dividends, and Dividend Reinvestment Plan (DRIP). Shareholders who own the stock on the record date will receive the dividend payment.

THE IMPACT OF DIVIDENDS ON STOCK PRICES

Dividends can have a significant impact on the price of a stock. The relationship between dividends and stock prices is complex and multifaceted and is influenced by a variety of factors such as the company's financial performance, the overall economic environment, and investor sentiment.

One of the most important factors that affect the relationship between dividends and stock prices is the company's financial performance. Companies that have strong financial performance and are expected to continue growing their earnings are more likely to pay dividends and to increase their dividends over time. This can lead to an increase in the stock price as investors are willing to pay more for a stock that has a strong growth prospect and a stable dividend income.

Another important factor that affects the relationship between dividends and stock prices is the overall economic environment. During times of economic growth and stability, dividends tend to be more stable and companies are more likely to pay dividends. This can lead to an increase in the stock price as investors are more willing to invest in a stable and growing economy. On the other hand, during times of economic uncertainty and recession, dividends tend to be more volatile and companies are less likely to pay dividends. This can lead to a decrease in the stock price as investors are more cautious and less willing to invest in a volatile and uncertain economy.

Investor sentiment is another key factor that affects the relationship between dividends and stock prices. Investors tend to have a positive sentiment towards companies that pay dividends, as dividends provide a stable and predictable stream of income. This can lead to an increase in the stock price as investors are willing to pay more for a stock that has a stable and predictable income stream. On the other hand, investors tend to have a negative sentiment towards companies that do not pay dividends, as these companies do not provide a stable and predictable stream of income. This can lead to a decrease in the stock price as investors are less willing to pay for a stock that does not have a stable and predictable income stream.

It's also worth noting that there is a school of thought that argues that dividends do not have a significant impact on stock prices and that the main driver of stock prices is a company's earnings growth. This theory suggests that investors are more interested in a company's future earnings potential than in its current dividends.

In conclusion, the relationship between dividends and stock prices is complex and multifaceted and is influenced by a variety of factors such as the company's financial performance, the overall economic environment, and investor sentiment. Companies with strong financial performance and stable growth prospects tend to pay dividends and increase them over time, leading to an increase in the stock price. Dividends can be a stable and predictable stream of income for investors, which can lead to an increase in the stock price. However, the general economic environment and investor sentiment also play a role. Some argue that dividends are not the main driver of stock prices and that earnings growth is the most important factor.

CHAPTER 3: DIVIDEND INVESTING STRATEGIES

Dividend investing is a popular strategy among investors who are looking for a steady stream of income from their investments. By focusing on companies that pay dividends, investors can benefit from regular cash payments, as well as the potential for capital appreciation over time. However, there are many different ways to approach dividend investing, and it's important to understand the different strategies that are available in order to make the most of your investment.

In this chapter, we will explore some of the most popular dividend investing strategies, including dividend growth investing, dividend income investing, and dividend yield investing. We will also discuss the pros and cons of each strategy, and how to determine which strategy is right for you based on your investment goals and risk tolerance. Whether you're a beginner or an experienced investor, this chapter will provide valuable insights and practical tips for building a successful dividend investing portfolio.

DIVIDEND GROWTH INVESTING

Dividend growth investing is a strategy that focuses on investing in companies that have a history of consistently increasing their dividends over time. The idea behind this strategy is that companies that are able to consistently increase their dividends are financially strong and have stable growth prospects. By investing in these companies, investors can benefit from both a steady stream of income, as well as the potential for capital appreciation over time.

One of the main advantages of dividend growth investing is that it can provide a reliable and growing stream of income. As the dividends increase over time, the income from the investment also increases, which can be particularly beneficial for investors in retirement or those looking for income from their investments. In addition, companies that consistently increase their dividends are often financially strong and have stable growth prospects, which can lead to capital appreciation over time.

When selecting stocks for a dividend growth portfolio, investors usually focus on companies that have a track record of consistent and growing dividends, a strong financial position, and promising future growth prospects. This can include companies in stable and defensive industries such as utilities, consumer staples, and healthcare. Additionally, investors tend to look for companies that have a low payout ratio, which means that the company is not paying out a large portion of its earnings as dividends and have room to grow its dividends.

It's also worth noting that dividend growth investing is a long-term strategy and it may take several years before the dividends and the stock price starts to grow. Additionally, dividend growth stocks tend to be less volatile than other stocks, which can be beneficial for investors who are risk-averse.

In conclusion, dividend growth investing is a strategy that focuses on investing in companies that have a history of consistently increasing their dividends over time. This can provide a reliable and growing stream of income, as well as the potential for capital appreciation over time. Dividend growth investing is a long-term strategy that can be beneficial for investors who are looking for a stable and growing income stream and are willing to hold their investments for an extended period. It's also important to note that investors tend to look for companies that have a strong financial position and promising future growth prospects when building a dividend growth portfolio.

DIVIDEND INCOME INVESTING

Dividend income investing is a strategy that focuses on investing in companies that pay high dividends, with the goal of generating a steady stream of income from the dividends. This strategy is popular among investors who are looking for a reliable source of income, such as retirees or those who are looking to supplement their income.

One of the main advantages of dividend income investing is that it can provide a steady stream of income. By investing in companies that pay high dividends, investors can receive regular cash payments, which can be used for living expenses or to invest in other income-generating assets. Additionally, companies that pay high dividends tend to be financially stable and have a strong business model, which can lead to capital appreciation over time.

When selecting stocks for a dividend income portfolio, investors usually focus on companies that have a high dividend yield, which is the annual dividend per share divided by the stock price. Additionally, investors tend to look for companies that have a consistent and long history of paying dividends and a low payout ratio, which means that the company is not paying out a large portion of its earnings as dividends and has room to grow its dividends.

It's also worth noting that dividend income investing is a long-term strategy and it may take several years before dividends and the stock price starts to grow. Additionally, dividend-income stocks tend to be less volatile than other stocks, which can be beneficial for investors who are risk-averse.

In conclusion, dividend income investing is a strategy that focuses on investing in companies that pay high dividends with the goal of generating a steady stream of income. This strategy is popular among investors who are looking for a reliable source of income and are willing to hold their investments for an extended period. When selecting stocks for a dividend income portfolio, investors usually focus on companies that have a high dividend yield, a consistent and long history of paying dividends, and a low payout ratio. Additionally, it's worth noting that dividend income investing is a long-term strategy and it may take several years before dividends and the stock price starts to grow.

DIVIDEND YIELD INVESTING

Dividend yield investing is a strategy that focuses on investing in companies that have a high dividend yield, which is the annual dividend per share divided by the stock price. The goal of this strategy is to generate a high return on investment from the dividends received.

One of the main advantages of dividend yield investing is that it can provide a high return on investment. Companies that have a high dividend yield tend to pay out a large portion of their earnings as dividends, which can provide a significant return for investors. Additionally, companies that have a high dividend yield tend to be financially stable and have a strong business model, which can lead to capital appreciation over time.

When selecting stocks for a dividend yield portfolio, investors usually focus on companies that have a high dividend yield, which can be found by dividing the annual dividend per share by the stock price. Additionally, investors tend to look for companies that have a consistent and long history of paying dividends and a low payout ratio, which means that the company is not paying out a large portion of its earnings as dividends and has room to grow its dividends.

It's important to note that dividend yield investing can be a high-risk strategy and investors should be aware that high-yield stocks may be more susceptible to market fluctuations. Additionally, while a high-yield stock may appear to be a great investment opportunity, it's important to consider the company's financial stability and future growth prospects.

In conclusion, dividend yield investing is a strategy that focuses on investing in companies that have a high dividend yield, with the goal of generating a high return on investment from the dividends received. This strategy is popular among investors who are looking for a high return on investment and are willing to take on higher risk. When selecting stocks for a dividend yield portfolio, investors usually focus on companies that have a high dividend yield, a consistent and long history of paying dividends, and a low payout ratio. However, it's important to note that high-yield stocks may be more susceptible to market fluctuations and investors should be aware of the company's financial stability and future growth prospects.

SELECTING THE RIGHT DIVIDEND INVESTING STRATEGY - AT A GLANCE

Dividend investing is a popular strategy for generating income from stocks. However, there are different strategies to choose from, each with its own advantages and disadvantages. So which should you choose?

Dividend growth investing is a strategy that focuses on investing in companies that have a history of consistently increasing their dividends over time. The goal of this strategy is to generate long-term capital appreciation and a growing income stream. Companies that consistently increase their dividends are often financially stable and have a strong business model, which can lead to capital appreciation over time.

Dividend income investing is a strategy that focuses on investing in companies that have a high current dividend yield and a consistent history of paying dividends. The goal of this strategy is to generate a high-income stream from the dividends received. Companies that have a high dividend yield tend to pay out a large portion of their earnings as dividends, which can provide a significant return for investors. However, it's important to consider the company's financial stability and future growth prospects, as high-yield stocks may be more susceptible to market fluctuations.

Dividend yield investing is a strategy that focuses on investing in companies that have a high dividend yield. The goal of this strategy is to generate a high return on investment from the dividends received. Companies that have a high dividend yield tend to be financially stable and have a strong business model, which can lead to capital appreciation over time. However, it's important to consider the company's financial stability and future growth prospects, as high-yield stocks may be more susceptible to market fluctuations.

When selecting a dividend investing strategy, it's important to consider your investment goals, risk tolerance, and time horizon. If you're looking for long-term capital appreciation and a growing income stream, dividend growth investing may be the best strategy for you. If you're looking for a high-income stream from dividends, dividend income investing may be the best strategy. And if you're looking for a high return on investment from dividends, dividend yield investing may be the best strategy for you.

It's also important to note that diversification is key, it's crucial to not put all your eggs in one basket, by having a portfolio that is diversified across different sectors, industries, and strategies. Dividend stocks can provide a steady stream of income, but it's important to have a well-diversified portfolio that includes other types of investments such as bonds, real estate, and cash.

When it comes to selecting the right dividend investing strategy, it's important to consider your investment goals, risk tolerance, and time horizon. Dividend growth investing, dividend income investing, and dividend yield investing are all popular strategies with their own advantages and disadvantages. It's important to do your research and consider the company's financial stability and future growth prospects before making any investment decisions. And it's also important to diversify your portfolio across different sectors, industries, and strategies.

CHAPTER 4: RISK MANAGEMENT AND DIVIDEND INVESTING

Dividend investing is a popular strategy for generating income from stocks. However, like any investment strategy, there is always a level of risk involved. It's important for investors to understand the risks associated with dividend investing and to implement risk management techniques to mitigate those risks.

In this chapter, we will explore the various risks associated with dividend investing, including interest rate risk, credit risk, and market risk. We will also discuss the importance of diversifying your portfolio and implementing risk management techniques such as stop-loss orders and hedging.

Investors should keep in mind that dividends are not guaranteed, and even companies with a long history of paying dividends can cut or eliminate them at any time, especially in times of economic stress. It's important to consider the company's financial stability and future growth prospects before making any investment decisions. Additionally, investors should also be aware of the potential risks associated with dividend-paying stocks and take appropriate measures to manage those risks.

By understanding the risks associated with dividend investing and implementing risk management techniques, investors can better protect their portfolios and maximize their returns. This chapter will provide an in-depth look at the various risks associated with dividend investing and the tools and strategies that can be used to manage those risks.

RISKS ASSOCIATED WITH DIVIDEND INVESTING

One of the main risks associated with dividend investing is interest rate risk. When interest rates rise, the value of dividend-paying stocks may decrease. This is because as interest rates rise, the return on fixed-income investments such as bonds becomes more attractive, making stocks less appealing. This can lead to a decrease in demand for stocks and a decrease in stock prices.

Another risk associated with dividend investing is credit risk. Credit risk refers to the risk that a company may not be able to make its dividend payments. This can occur if a company experiences financial difficulties, such as a decrease in revenue or an increase in debt. If a company is unable to make its dividend payments, investors may lose a portion of their investment.

Market risk is another risk associated with dividend investing. Market risk refers to the risk that the overall stock market will decline, which can lead to a decrease in the value of dividend-paying stocks. This risk can be caused by a variety of factors, including economic downturns, political instability, and natural disasters.

Dividend risk is also associated with dividend investing. Dividend risk refers to the risk that a company may cut or eliminate its dividends. This can occur if a company experiences financial difficulties or if it decides to use its earnings for other purposes, such as reinvesting in the business or paying off debt.

To manage these risks, investors should diversify their portfolios and invest in a variety of dividend-paying stocks, including blue-chip stocks, REITs, and MLPs. Additionally, investors should also be aware of the potential risks associated with dividend-paying stocks and take appropriate measures to manage those risks. This can include using stop-loss orders and hedging strategies to limit losses.

In addition, investors should also consider the company's financial stability and future growth prospects before making any investment decisions. It's also important to keep in mind that dividends are not guaranteed and even companies with a long history of paying dividends can cut or eliminate them at any time, especially in times of economic stress.

Overall, dividend investing can be a great way to generate income from stocks, but it's important to understand and manage the risks associated with this strategy. By understanding the risks and implementing risk management techniques, investors can better protect their portfolios and maximize their returns.

MANAGING RISKS IN DIVIDEND INVESTING

Dividend investing can be a great way to generate income from stocks, but it's important to understand and manage the risks associated with this strategy. In this chapter, we will discuss various techniques that investors can use to manage the risks associated with dividend investing.

Diversification

Diversification is one of the most important techniques for managing risks in dividend investing. Diversification refers to the practice of investing in a variety of different stocks, sectors, and industries. By diversifying your portfolio, you can reduce the risk of losing all your investment due to the poor performance of a single stock or sector.

One way to diversify your portfolio is to invest in a variety of different dividend-paying stocks, such as blue-chip stocks, REITs, and MLPs. This will help to spread the risk of losing money due to the poor performance of a single stock or sector. Additionally, investors can also invest in a variety of different sectors and industries, such as healthcare, technology, and consumer goods.

Monitoring Dividend Payments

Another technique for managing risks in dividend investing is monitoring dividend payments. This includes keeping track of when dividends are paid, how much they are, and whether they are increasing or decreasing. By monitoring dividend payments, investors can better understand the financial stability of a company and whether it is likely to continue paying dividends in the future.

Investors can also use stop-loss orders to manage risks in dividend investing. A stop-loss order is a type of order that is placed with a broker to sell a stock when it reaches a certain price. This can help to limit losses if the stock's price falls below a certain level.

Hedging strategies can also be used to manage risks in dividend investing. Hedging refers to the practice of using financial instruments, such as options or futures, to offset the risk of a potential loss. For example, an investor can purchase put options on a stock to offset the risk of losing money due to a decrease in the stock's price.

Overall, there are several techniques that investors can use to manage the risks associated with dividend investing. By diversifying their portfolios, monitoring dividend payments, using stop-loss orders, and implementing hedging strategies, investors can better protect their portfolios and maximize their returns.

It's also important to keep in mind that managing risks doesn't mean avoiding them completely. Some level of risk is inherent to any investment, and investors should be comfortable with the amount of risk they are taking on. It's important to remember that the aim is to balance the potential returns with the potential risks, so investors can reach their financial goals.

CHAPTER 5: TAX IMPLICATIONS OF DIVIDEND INVESTING

Always consult a professional before making any decisions regarding calculating and paying taxes.

Dividend investing can be a great way to generate income from stocks, but it's important to understand the tax implications of this strategy. In this chapter, we will discuss various tax implications that investors need to be aware of when investing in dividend-paying stocks.

The first thing to understand is that dividends are considered taxable income by the IRS. This means that investors will have to pay taxes on any dividends they receive from their investments. The tax rate on dividends is generally lower than the tax rate on ordinary income, but it still needs to be taken into account when planning for taxes.

There are two types of dividends: qualified and non-qualified. Qualified dividends are taxed at the lower capital gains tax rate, which is typically lower than the tax rate on ordinary income. Non-qualified dividends, on the other hand, are taxed at the higher ordinary income tax rate.

To be considered a qualified dividend, the dividend must meet certain criteria. These include the requirement that the stock is held for more than 60 days during the 121-day period that begins 60 days before the ex-dividend date. Additionally, the dividend must be paid by a U.S. corporation or a qualifying foreign corporation.

Another important tax implication to consider is the impact of dividends on the cost basis of a stock. When a stock pays a dividend, the cost basis of the stock is reduced by the amount of the dividend. This means that when the stock is sold, the capital gain or loss will be calculated based on the reduced cost basis.

Investors should also be aware of the tax implications of reinvesting dividends. Many companies allow investors to automatically reinvest dividends, but this can have tax implications. When dividends are reinvested, the cost basis of the stock is increased by the amount of the dividend, which can increase the capital gain or loss when the stock is sold.

It is also important to be aware of the tax implications of dividends when investing in different types of stocks. For example, REITs and MLPs often pay out a high percentage of their earnings as dividends, but these dividends may be considered as a return of capital, which can have different tax implications.

Overall, the tax implications of dividend investing are important to consider when planning your investment strategy. By understanding the different types of dividends, the impact of dividends on the cost basis of a stock, and the tax implications of reinvesting dividends, investors can better plan for taxes and maximize their returns.

It is also important to consult with a tax professional when dealing with tax implications, especially when it comes to reporting, as tax laws and rules may vary depending on the country or state and the circumstances.

MINIMIZING TAXES ON DIVIDENDS

One of the key benefits of investing in dividend-paying stocks is the regular income they provide. However, it is important to consider the tax implications of these dividends, as they are generally considered taxable income. We will discuss the various ways to minimize the tax burden on dividend income.

First, it is important to understand the tax treatment of dividends in your country. In many countries, dividends are taxed at a lower rate than other forms of income, but there are still taxes that must be paid. It is important to understand the tax laws in your country and consult with a financial advisor or tax professional if necessary.

Another way to minimize taxes on dividends is

through tax-deferred accounts, such as individual retirement accounts (IRAs) or 401(k)s. In these types of accounts, taxes are deferred until the funds are withdrawn, which can significantly reduce the tax burden. Additionally, many countries offer special tax incentives for investing in dividend-paying stocks, such as tax credits or deductions.

Dividend reinvestment plans (DRIPs) can also be a tax-efficient way to invest in dividend-paying stocks. With a DRIP, dividends are automatically reinvested in the stock, rather than being paid out in cash. This can help to reduce the amount of taxable income, as there is no cash transaction to report.

Finally, it is important to consider the timing of dividend payments. Dividends are typically paid on a regular schedule, such as quarterly or annually. If you are in a high tax bracket, it may be advantageous to time your investments so that you receive dividends in a lower tax bracket year. This can be done by selling stocks that have recently paid dividends and then purchasing new stocks after the dividend payment date.

There are several strategies that can be used to minimize taxes on dividends, including understanding the tax laws in your country, utilizing tax-deferred accounts, participating in dividend reinvestment plans, and carefully timing dividend payments. By understanding these strategies, investors can maximize the benefits of investing in dividend-paying stocks while minimizing the tax burden.

ANALYSIS OF HOW TAX LAWS AND REGULATIONS AFFECT DIVIDEND INVESTING

We will now delve into the impact that tax laws and regulations have on dividend investing. Understanding the tax implications of investing in dividend-paying stocks is an important aspect of building a well-rounded investment strategy.

Taxation of Dividends:

Dividends are taxed differently from capital gains,

which are profits from selling stocks at a higher price than what was paid for them. Dividends are considered income and are taxed as such, which means that the investor will be subject to their regular income tax rate. The tax rate for dividends depends on the tax bracket of the investor and can vary between countries and jurisdictions.

Qualified vs. Non-Qualified Dividends:

In the United States, there are two types of dividends: qualified and non-qualified. Qualified dividends are taxed at a lower rate than non-qualified dividends, making them more attractive to investors. To be considered a qualified dividend, the stock must meet certain criteria, such as being held for a certain period of time, and the dividend must come from a U.S. corporation or a qualifying foreign corporation.

International Dividend Investing:

Investing in international dividend-paying stocks can also have tax implications. In some cases, foreign taxes may be levied on the dividends, and the investor may also be subject to U.S. taxes on their foreign dividends. It is important for investors to be aware of the tax laws and regulations of the country in which the stock is based, as well as the tax laws and regulations of their own country.

Dividend Reinvestment Plans (DRIPs):

As mentioned previously Dividend reinvestment

plans (DRIPs) allow investors to automatically reinvest their dividends into additional shares of the same stock, rather than receiving the dividend as cash. This can be a tax-efficient way to grow a portfolio, as the reinvested dividends will increase the cost basis of the stock, reducing the capital gains tax that would be owed if the stock were sold.

Tax laws and regulations play a significant role in dividend investing, and it is essential for investors to understand the tax implications of their investment decisions. Investors should always consult with a financial advisor and a tax professional to ensure that their investment strategy is tax-efficient and aligns with their overall financial goals. By taking the time to understand the tax laws and regulations affecting their investments, investors can make informed decisions and maximize their returns over the long term.

CHAPTER 6: THE IMPACT OF LOW-INTEREST RATES ON DIVIDEND INVESTING

In recent years, many investors have been drawn to dividend-paying stocks as a way to generate a steady stream of income in a low-interest-rate environment. The global economy has experienced a period of low-interest rates, leading many investors to consider how this trend might impact dividend investing. In this chapter, we will examine the relationship between low-interest rates and dividend investing and discuss the implications for individual investors.

Understanding Low-Interest Rates

Low interest rates refer to the level of interest that banks and other financial institutions offer on their deposits and loans. A low-interest-rate environment means that borrowing costs are low, and it becomes easier for consumers and businesses to access credit. Central banks set interest rates to help control inflation, regulate the supply of money in the economy, and support economic growth.

The Relationship between Low-Interest Rates and Dividend Investing

In a low-interest-rate environment, many investors find dividend-paying stocks more attractive because they offer a higher yield than traditional fixed-income investments such as bonds. Low-interest rates reduce the yield of bonds, making them less attractive to income-seeking investors. As a result, many investors turn to dividend-paying stocks, which offer the potential for higher yields and the potential for capital appreciation.

The Implications for Investors

While low-interest rates may increase the appeal of dividend-paying stocks, they also pose some risks for investors. For example, low-interest rates can increase competition among investors for high-yielding stocks, pushing prices higher and reducing potential returns. Additionally, low-interest rates can increase the risk of inflation, which could erode the value of any income received from dividend-paying stocks.

Low-interest rates can have a significant impact on dividend investing. While they may increase the appeal of dividend-paying stocks, they also present some risks that investors should be aware of. It is essential for investors to understand the relationship between low-interest rates and dividend investing and to make informed investment decisions that align with their investment goals and risk tolerance. By diversifying their portfolios and regularly monitoring their investments, investors can help minimize their risk and maximize their returns in a low-interest-rate environment.

FINDING DIVIDEND-PAYING STOCKS IN A LOW-INTEREST RATE ENVIRONMENT

In a low-interest rate environment, many investors are searching for ways to generate income from their investments. This chapter will explore how to find dividend-paying stocks in a low-interest-rate environment.

1. Identify the right type of stocks: One of the first steps in finding dividend-paying stocks is to identify the right type of stocks.

Companies in mature industries such as utilities, consumer goods, and healthcare are typically more likely to pay dividends.

2. Use stock screening tools: Another way to find dividend-paying stocks is to use stock screening tools. Many financial websites offer free screening tools that allow investors to search for stocks based on specific criteria such as dividend yield, payout ratio, and dividend growth rate.

3. Research the company's financials: Once you have identified a potential dividend-paying stock, it is important to research the company's financials. Look for companies with a solid track record of paying dividends, a strong balance sheet, and a history of stable earnings.

4. Consider the company's dividend history: The company's dividend history is also important when searching for dividend-paying stocks. A company that has consistently paid dividends over a long period of time is more likely to continue to pay dividends in the future.

5. Monitor changes in the interest rate environment: Finally, it is important to monitor changes in the interest rate environment. As interest rates rise, it may become more difficult to find high-

yielding dividend-paying stocks. Investors should be prepared to adjust their portfolios accordingly if interest rates rise.

Finding dividend-paying stocks in a low-interest-rate environment can be challenging, but with the right approach, it is possible. By using stock screening tools, researching the company's financials, and monitoring changes in the interest rate environment, investors can increase their chances of finding high-yielding dividend-paying stocks.

BOND AND FIXED INCOME INVESTMENTS IN A DIVIDEND INVESTING STRATEGY

We will now examine the role of bonds and other fixed-income investments in a dividend investing strategy. Low-interest rates have been a persistent concern for investors in recent years, making it more challenging to generate income from traditional sources. As a result, many investors are turning to dividend-paying stocks as an alternative source of income. But, combining bonds and other fixed-income investments with dividend-paying stocks can provide a well-rounded income portfolio, reducing risk while providing a steady stream of income.

Explanation of Bonds and Fixed Income Investments:

Bonds and fixed-income investments are financial instruments that offer a fixed rate of return, making them a popular choice for conservative investors seeking steady income. When you buy a bond, you are essentially lending money to a company or government, and in return, they promise to pay you a fixed interest rate for a specified period. Fixed-income investments can also include money market funds, CDs, and annuities.

Benefits of Including Bonds in a Dividend Investing Strategy:

Adding bonds and other fixed-income investments to a dividend investing strategy provides a few key benefits:

1. Diversification: By including bonds in your portfolio, you can reduce your overall investment risk by spreading your investments across multiple asset classes.

2. Income stability: Bonds provide a consistent and stable source of income, which can be particularly useful in a low-interest-rate environment.

3. Interest rate risk mitigation: With fixed-income investments, the risk of changes in interest rates is mitigated. If interest rates rise, bond prices will likely fall, but the fixed income stream from bonds can help offset this loss.

Examination of Bond and Fixed Income Investment Options:

There are a variety of bond and fixed-income investment options available to investors, each with its own unique characteristics and risk levels. Some of the most popular options include:

1. Corporate Bonds: Corporate bonds are issued by companies seeking to raise capital. They offer higher yields than government bonds, but also carry a higher risk.

2. Municipal Bonds: Municipal bonds are issued by state and local governments and are tax-free, making them an attractive option for income-seeking investors in high tax brackets.

3. Treasury Bonds: Treasury bonds are issued by the U.S. government and are considered the safest type of bond. They offer lower yields but are a secure source of income.

4. Money Market Funds: Money market funds invest in short-term, highly liquid debt

instruments and offer a low-risk source of income.

Including bonds and other fixed-income investments in a dividend investing strategy can provide stability and diversification to a portfolio, reducing risk while providing a steady stream of income. With a variety of options available, investors can tailor their bond and fixed-income investment portfolio to meet their individual goals and risk tolerance. By combining dividend-paying stocks with bonds and other fixed-income investments, investors can create a well-rounded income portfolio that can help meet their long-term financial goals.

CHAPTER 7: DIVIDEND INVESTING IN INTERNATIONAL MARKETS

Dividend investing is not just limited to the domestic markets, it can also be extended to international markets. With the globalization of the economy and the increasing interconnectedness of the world's financial markets, it's becoming increasingly popular for investors to explore dividend investment opportunities in foreign countries.

Investing in international markets can provide investors with access to a wider range of stocks and a diversified portfolio, which can help to reduce investment risk. It can also provide investors with the opportunity to capitalize on growth and income from markets that are not well-represented in the domestic market.

In this chapter, we will examine the opportunities and challenges of dividend investing in international markets. We will explore the different types of international stocks that pay dividends, and how to research and select stocks from international markets. We will also discuss the tax implications and the risks associated with investing in international markets.

Overall, this chapter will provide a comprehensive overview of the benefits and risks of dividend investing in international markets and help investors to make informed decisions about expanding their investment portfolio to include foreign dividend-paying stocks.

FINDING AND RESEARCHING INTERNATIONAL DIVIDEND-PAYING STOCKS

Investing in international dividend-paying stocks can be a great way to diversify your investment portfolio and potentially earn additional income. However, finding and researching international stocks can be a challenge, particularly for investors who are new to the process.

In this chapter, we will provide a step-by-step guide on how to find and research international dividend-paying stocks.

Step 1: Define Your Investment Goals

Before you start searching for international dividend-paying stocks, it's important to define your investment goals. This will help you determine the types of stocks that are best suited to your needs. For example, are you looking for a steady income stream or long-term growth? Do you have a particular geographic region or industry sector in mind?

Step 2: Use Online Resources

There are numerous online resources available that can help you find and research international dividend-paying stocks. Websites such as Yahoo Finance, Google Finance, and the websites of stock exchanges in other countries are a good place to start. You can use these websites to find stocks that are listed on foreign stock exchanges and to research the stocks' dividend history and other financial information.

Step 3: Analyze The Company's Financials

Once you have found a stock that you're interested in, it's important to analyze the company's financials to determine if it's a good investment. This includes reviewing the company's balance sheet, income statement, and cash flow statement. Look for red flags such as declining revenue or earnings, high debt levels, or declining dividend payments.

Step 4: Consider The Political And Economic Environment

When investing in international dividend-paying stocks, it's important to consider the political and economic environment of the country in which the company operates. This includes factors such as the stability of the government, the state of the economy, and the impact of exchange rate fluctuations on the stock's value.

Step 5: Diversify Your Portfolio

Finally, it's important to diversify your portfolio by investing in a range of international dividend-paying stocks. This will help to reduce your investment risk and ensure that you're not overly exposed to any one stock or market.

By following these steps, you can find and research international dividend-paying stocks with confidence, and make informed investment decisions.

DIVERSIFYING YOUR DIVIDEND PORTFOLIO WITH INTERNATIONAL STOCKS

Investing in international stocks is a way to diversify your portfolio and potentially increase your returns. The idea behind diversification is to spread your investment across different industries, countries, and currencies to reduce the overall risk of your portfolio. When it comes to dividend investing, international stocks offer a unique opportunity to achieve this goal.

We will now discuss the importance of diversifying your dividend portfolio with international stocks.

We will also provide a step-by-step guide on how to find and research international dividend-paying stocks to help you make informed investment decisions.

First, it's important to understand the benefits of investing in international stocks. By investing in companies in different countries, you can tap into different economies and markets that may offer higher growth potential or stability. Additionally, international stocks can provide exposure to currencies other than the US dollar, which can help to protect against fluctuations in the exchange rate.

When it comes to finding international dividend-paying stocks, there are several resources you can use. One of the best places to start is by researching the stock markets of countries that interest you. This may involve reading financial news articles, looking at economic indicators, and reviewing financial reports from companies in the region.

Once you have identified a few countries that interest you, you can start looking for dividend-paying stocks in those markets. You can do this by searching online databases and financial websites, as well as reading analyst reports and articles from financial advisors.

By following this process, you can find and research international dividend-paying stocks to add to your portfolio. Diversifying with international stocks can help you achieve a more balanced portfolio and potentially increase your returns over time.

CHAPTER 8: THE DIVIDEND SNOWBALL - THE POWER OF COMPOUND DIVIDEND GROWTH

One of the key benefits of dividend investing is the potential for compounding returns over time. This chapter will explore the concept of the "dividend snowball" and how reinvesting dividends can lead to exponential growth in wealth over the long term.

WHAT IS THE DIVIDEND SNOWBALL?

The dividend snowball refers to the process of reinvesting dividends in order to generate additional income over time. Essentially, when a stock pays a dividend, the investor can choose to either receive that income in cash or reinvest it by purchasing additional shares of the stock. By reinvesting the dividends, the investor is able to increase their exposure to the underlying stock, which can lead to increased dividends in the future. This process repeats itself over time, leading to a cumulative effect that can result in significant growth.

THE POWER OF COMPOUND GROWTH:

The dividend snowball is a prime example of the power of compounding. Compounding is the process by which an investment's returns generate additional income over time. The longer the investment is held and the more frequently the income is reinvested, the greater the potential for compounding. In the case of the dividend snowball, the reinvestment of dividends leads to the generation of more dividends, which can then be reinvested to generate even more income. This cumulative effect can result in exponential growth over time.

EXAMPLES OF THE DIVIDEND SNOWBALL:

To illustrate the power of the dividend snowball, let's consider an example. Suppose an investor has $10,000 invested in a stock that pays a 4% dividend yield. If the investor reinvests their dividends, over the course of 20 years, their investment would grow to over $23,000, assuming no other changes in the stock price or dividend yield. This growth is due solely to the compounding of the reinvested dividends.

THE IMPORTANCE OF REINVESTING DIVIDENDS:

The dividend snowball highlights the importance of reinvesting dividends, particularly for long-term investors. By reinvesting dividends, an investor is able to take advantage of the compounding effect and potentially increase their wealth over time. Additionally, reinvesting dividends can help to smooth out the ups and downs of the stock market by providing a steady stream of income.

The dividend snowball is a powerful concept that highlights the potential for compounding returns through the reinvestment of dividends. By taking advantage of this process, investors can potentially increase their wealth over the long term. Whether an investor is focused on dividend growth, dividend income, or the dividend yield, the reinvestment of dividends can play an important role in their investment strategy.

CHAPTER 9: WHY WARREN BUFFET LOVES DIVIDENDS

Warren Buffet is widely regarded as one of the most successful investors of all time, and his investing philosophy has been studied and analyzed by millions of people worldwide. One of the key tenets of Buffet's investment philosophy is his love for dividends, which he has referred to as the "miracle of compounding."

In this chapter, we will examine why Buffet is so enamored with dividends and why they play such an important role in his investment strategy. To begin, it is important to understand what dividends are and why they are important to stock investors.

Dividends are payments made by companies to their shareholders, usually in the form of cash or additional stock. The purpose of these payments is to reward shareholders for investing in the company and to provide a return on their investment. Dividends are an important source of income for many investors, and they are often viewed as a way to stabilize the price of a stock.

For Buffet, the appeal of dividends lies in their ability to compound over time. In other words, the more dividends a stock pays, the more its value increases. This is because the additional income generated by the dividends can be reinvested, which in turn generates more income and contributes to the growth of the stock.

In addition to the compounding benefits of dividends, Buffet also values the stability they bring to a portfolio. By investing in companies that pay dividends, Buffet is able to receive a regular stream of income, which helps to balance out any fluctuations in the stock market.

Finally, Buffet views dividends as a sign of a company's financial health. Companies that are able to pay dividends are typically generating steady profits, which is a positive indicator of their long-term prospects. By investing in these types of companies, Buffet is able to minimize his risk and increase his chances of success.

Warren Buffet's love for dividends is well-founded, and it is a testament to the power of compounding and the stability they bring to a portfolio. By understanding the reasons why Buffet values dividends so highly, individual investors can improve their own investment strategies and increase their chances of success.

CHAPTER 10: CONCLUSION - THE POWER OF DIVIDEND INVESTING

Dividend investing is a popular strategy among investors for generating steady income, building wealth, and reducing investment risk. Throughout this book, we have explored various aspects of dividend investing, including what dividends are, why they are important to stock investors, the different types of dividend-paying stocks, how dividends are calculated and paid out, the impact of dividends on stock prices, different dividend investing strategies, and the risks and tax implications associated with dividend investing.

We have discussed the importance of reinvesting dividends to maximize returns over time through the "dividend snowball" effect, as well as the ongoing research and trends in dividend investing. We have also explored why Warren Buffet, one of the world's most successful investors, is a big fan of dividends.

DISCUSSION OF ONGOING RESEARCH AND TRENDS IN DIVIDEND INVESTING

Dividend investing has been a popular strategy among investors for many years, and it continues to evolve and grow in popularity. As a result, there is a wealth of ongoing research and trends that are shaping the world of dividend investing.

In this chapter, we will discuss some of the key research and trends that are currently driving the world of dividend investing. To begin, it is important to understand that dividends are influenced by many different factors, including economic conditions, company performance, and regulatory changes.

One trend that is currently shaping the world of dividend investing is the increasing popularity of dividend growth investing. This approach focuses on investing in companies that have a history of consistently increasing their dividends over time. By investing in these types of companies, investors are able to benefit from the compounding effects of dividends, which can result in significant growth over time.

Another trend that is currently shaping the world of dividend investing is the increasing use of exchange-traded funds (ETFs) and other passive investment vehicles. These types of investment vehicles allow investors to easily access a diversified portfolio of dividend-paying stocks, which can help to mitigate risk and increase returns.

In addition to these trends, there is also ongoing research into the relationship between dividends and stock prices. This research is helping to shed light on the various factors that influence the value of a stock, including dividends, and it is providing investors with valuable insights into how they can make informed investment decisions.

Finally, there is also ongoing research into the

impact of taxes on dividends. As governments around the world continue to grapple with budget deficits and other financial challenges, many are looking at ways to increase tax revenues, including changes to the way dividends are taxed. This research is helping to provide investors with a better understanding of the tax implications of dividend investing and how they can optimize their portfolios to minimize their tax liability.

The world of dividend investing is constantly evolving and growing. There is a wealth of ongoing research and trends that are shaping the field. By staying informed and up-to-date on these developments, investors can improve their investment strategies and increase their chances of success.

FINAL THOUGHTS AND RECOMMENDATIONS FOR INVESTORS.

In conclusion, dividend investing is a sound strategy for anyone seeking to generate income and build wealth over the long term. By understanding the basics of dividends, researching different dividend-paying stocks, and adopting a suitable dividend investing strategy, investors can enjoy the benefits of regular income and stable returns from their portfolios. However, it's important to remember that dividend investing, like any investment strategy, comes with risks and it's essential to carefully monitor your portfolio and diversify your investments to manage these risks effectively.

In the end, the key to successful dividend investing is to have a well-researched and thought-out strategy, a long-term investment horizon, and a commitment to regular monitoring and adjusting your portfolio as needed. With these steps in place, dividend investing can be a powerful tool in building a secure and prosperous financial future.

AFTERWORD

Disclaimer: The author of this book is not a licensed financial professional and the information contained within is not intended to be taken as financial advice. Investing in stocks and other securities carries a risk of loss. Please consult a licensed financial advisor and conduct your own research before making any investment decisions.

It is also important to consult with a tax professional when dealing with tax implications of investing, especially when it comes to reporting, as tax laws and rules may vary depending on the country or state and the circumstances.

www.ingramcontent.com/pod-product-compliance
Lightning Source LLC
Chambersburg PA
CBHW050243220526
45465CB00002B/536